So Into Science!

# EXPLORING THE WEATHER

By Emmett Martin

Gareth Stevens PUBLISHING

**Please visit our website, www.garethstevens.com. For a free color catalog of all our high-quality books, call toll free 1-800-542-2595 or fax 1-877-542-2596.**

**Library of Congress Cataloging-in-Publication Data**

Names: Martin, Emmett, author.
Title: Exploring the weather / Emmett Martin.
Description: New York : Gareth Stevens Publishing, [2019] | Series: So into science! | Includes index.
Identifiers: LCCN 2018013148| ISBN 9781538228890 (library bound) | ISBN 9781538232101 (pbk.) | ISBN 9781538233085 (6 pack)
Subjects: LCSH: Meteorology–Juvenile literature. | Weather–Juvenile literature.
Classification: LCC QC981.3 .M3668 2019 | DDC 551.5–dc23
LC record available at https://lccn.loc.gov/2018013148

Published in 2019 by
**Gareth Stevens Publishing**
111 East 14th Street, Suite 349
New York, NY 10003



Editor: Therese Shea
Designer: Sarah Liddell

Photo credits: Cover, p. 1 Peter Gudella/Shutterstock.com; pp. 5, 13 (sun) AlinaMD/Shutterstock.com; pp. 7, 24 (thermometer) txking/Shutterstock.com; p. 9 Titood99/Shutterstock.com; p. 11 Alinute Silzeviciute/Shutterstock.com; p. 13 (park) Trong Nguyen/Shutterstock.com; p. 15 benemale/Shutterstock.com; p. 17 Romrodphoto/Shutterstock.com; p. 19 Anton Watman/Shutterstock.com; pp. 21, 24 (meteorologist) Joe Raedle/Staff/Getty Images News/Getty Images; p. 23 YukoF/Shutterstock.com.



Printed in the United States of America

CPSIA compliance information: Batch #CW19GS: For further information contact Gareth Stevens, New York, New York at 1-800-542-2595.

# Contents

Weather is what's happening in the air around us.

A thermometer tells us the temperature.

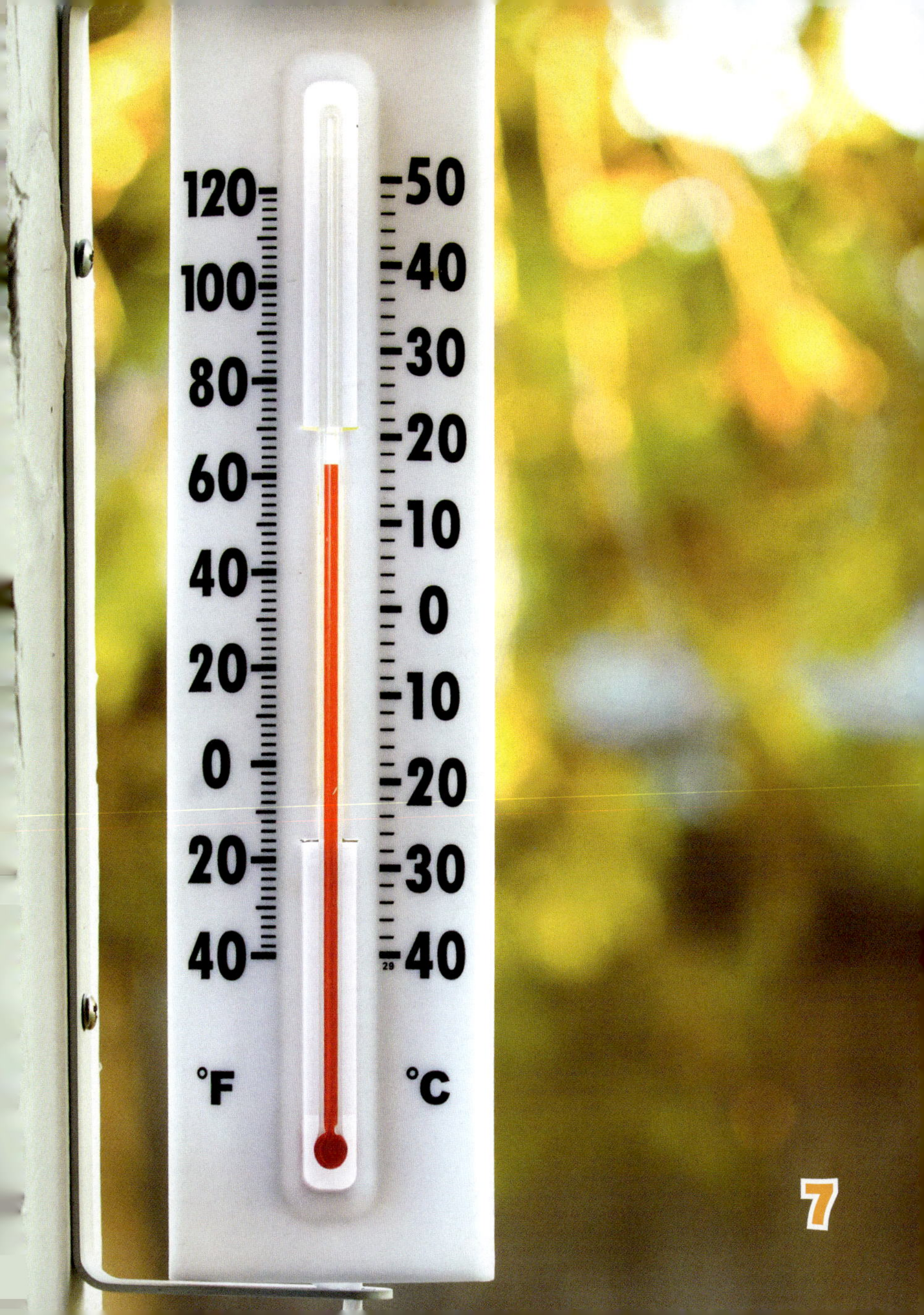
120
100
80
60
40
20
0
20
40
°F
50
40
30
20
10
0
10
20
30
40
°C

It's hot!
We go to the beach.

It's cold!
We ice-skate.

It’s sunny!
We go to the park.

STOP

It's windy!
We fly a kite.

It's raining!
We jump in puddles.

It's snowing!
We make snow angels.

Meteorologists are weather scientists. They tell us what the weather will be!

I have fun in all kinds of weather!

# Words to Know

meteorologist

thermometer

# Index